ØRJAN MATRE

Trompeten, Nacths und Untergang

for Trumpet in C and Choir (SSAATTBB)

(2020)

Vocal Score

EDITION PETERS

LEIPZIG · LONDON · NEW YORK

Commissioned by The Norwegian Soloists' Choir with support from Arts Council, Norway

1. Prelude

2. Spielen, tanzen, treiben

3. Trompeten

4. Interlude

5. Nachts

6. Untergang

(Total durata: Approximately 25 minutes)

Trompeten

Unter verschnittenen Weiden, wo braune Kinder spielen
Und Blätter treiben, tönen Trompeten. Ein Kirchhofsschauer.
Fahnen von Scharlach stürzen durch des Ahorns Trauer
Reiter entlang an Roggenfeldern, leeren Mühlen.

Oder Hirten singen nachts und Hirsche treten
In den Kreis ihrer Feuer, des Hains uralte Trauer,
Tanzende heben sich von einer schwarzen Mauer;
Fahnen von Scharlach, Lachen, Wahnsinn, Trompeten.

Nachts

Die Bläue meiner Augen ist erloschen in dieser Nacht,
Das rote Gold meines Herzens. O! wie stille brannte das Licht.
Dein blauer Mantel umfing den Sinkenden;
Dein roter Mund besiegelte des Freundes Umnachtung.

Untergang

Über den weißen Weiher
Sind die wilden Vögel fortgezogen.
Am Abend weht von unseren Sternen ein eisiger Wind.

Über unsere Gräber
Beugt sich die zerbrochene Stirne der Nacht.
Unter Eichen schaukeln wir auf einem silbernen Kahn.

Immer klingen die weißen Mauern der Stadt.
Unter Dornenbogen
O mein Bruder klimmen wir blinde Zeiger gen Mitternacht.

Georg Trakl (1887-1914)

Commissioned by The Norwegian Soloists' Choir

Trompeten, Nachts und Untergang

(2020)

1. Prelude

Ørjan Matre (b. 1979)
Text: Georg Trakl (1887-1914)

* The trumpet soloist should in the beginning of the piece be placed offstage, not visible to the audience.
The sound should be distant, but not *too* distant, with the trumpet fortissimo balancing the choir's mezzo-pianos.

Edition Peters 14530   34841   ©2020 by Henry Litolff's Verlag Ltd & Co. KG, Leipzig

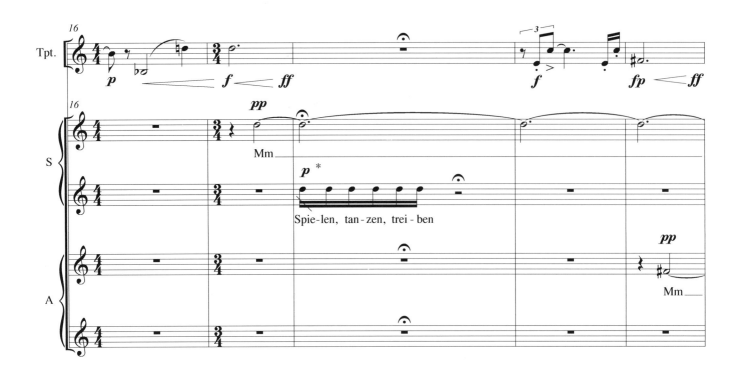

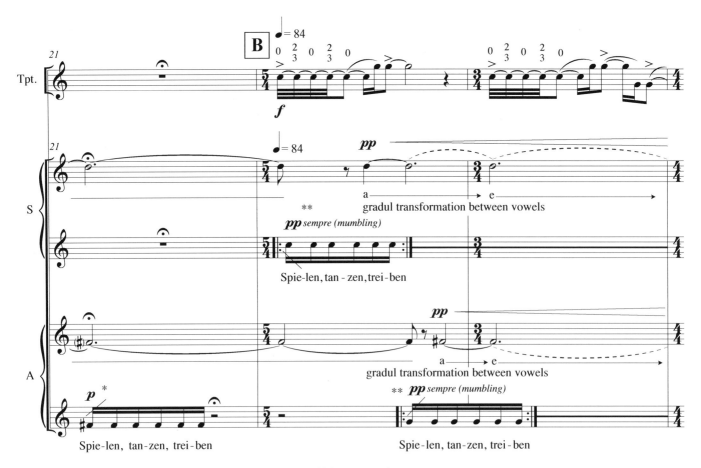

* Fast, free rythm. If more than one singer, the entries should be staggered.
** Repeat as long as the arrow indicates. If more than one singer, entries should be staggered.

6

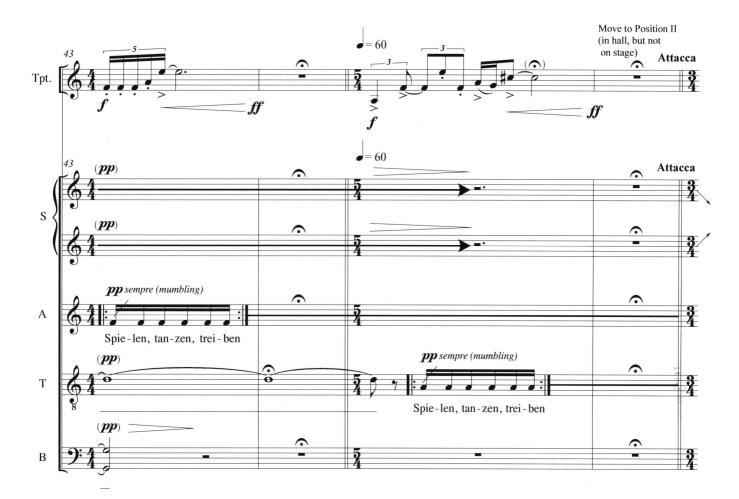

2. Spielen, tanzen, treiben

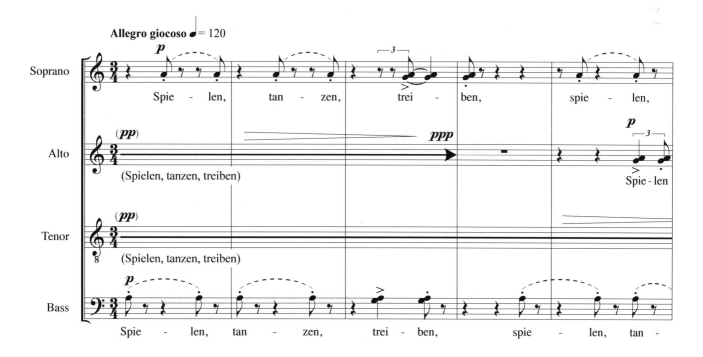

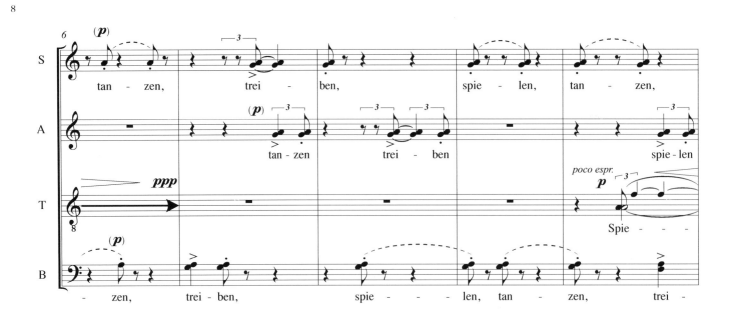

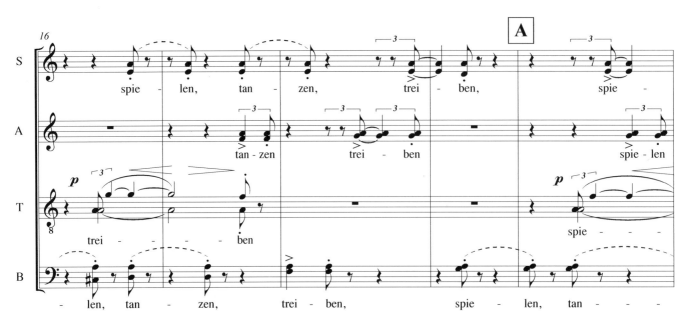

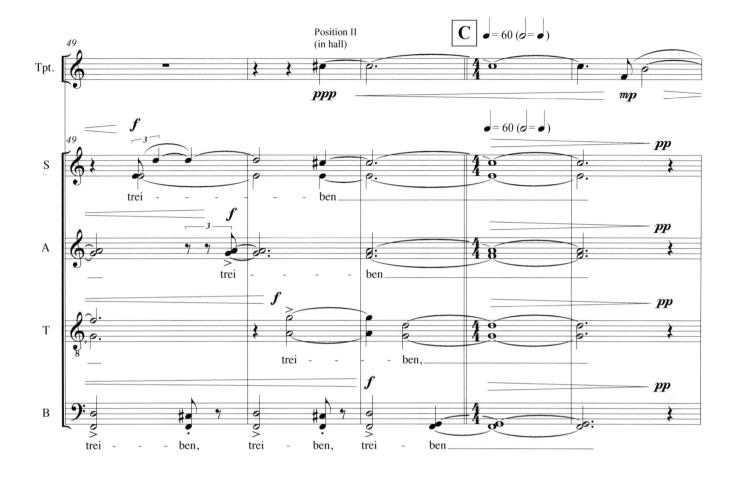

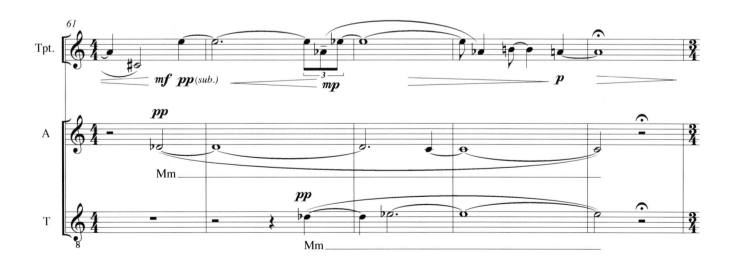

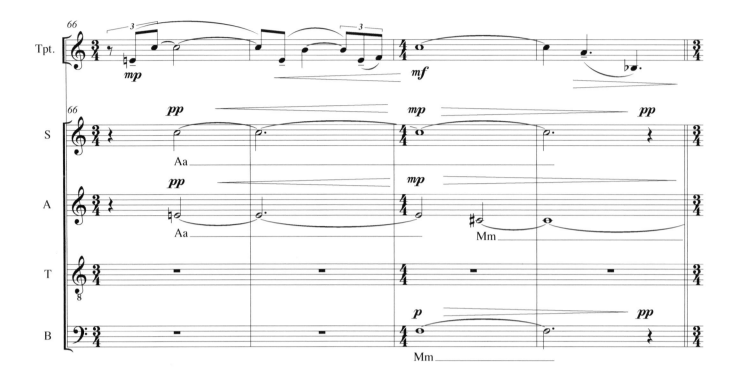

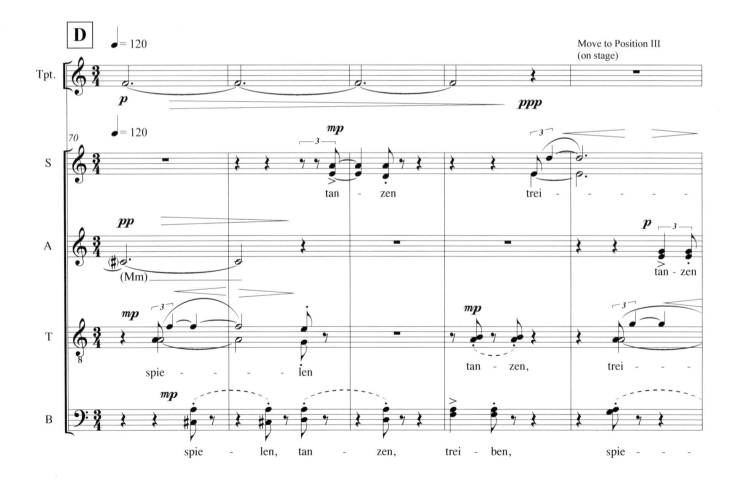

3. Trompeten

Position III
(on stage)
Straight mute
quasi lontano
18
Tpt.
S
ten
Trom - pe - - - - -
A
ten
Trom - pe - - - - - - ten
T
Mm
Trom - pe - - - - - ten
B
Trom - pe - - - - - - ten
23
Tpt.
S
ten
Trom - pe - - - - - ten
A
Ein Kirch - - - - - - hofs - schau - - - -
T
Mm
Trom - pe - - - - ten
B
Mm
Trom - pe - - - - ten

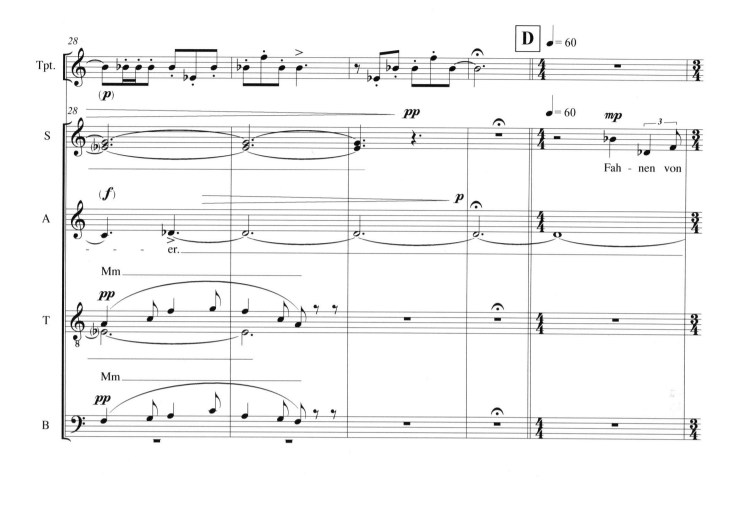

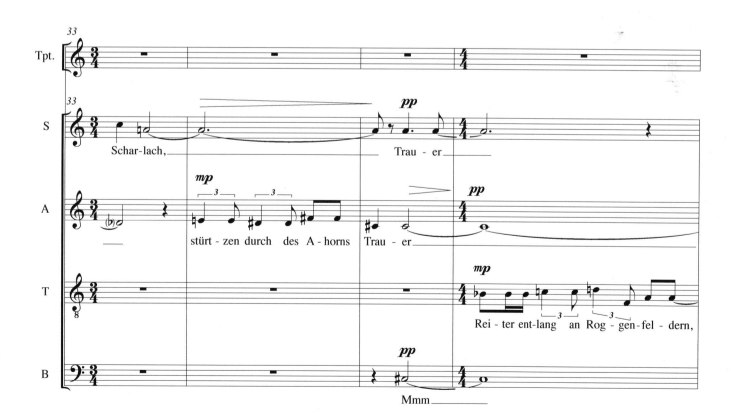

* If only eight singers, S2 can be omitted from second beat of bar 71 until bar 78. If none of the sopranos are able to sing the high C♯, the solo may be omitted.

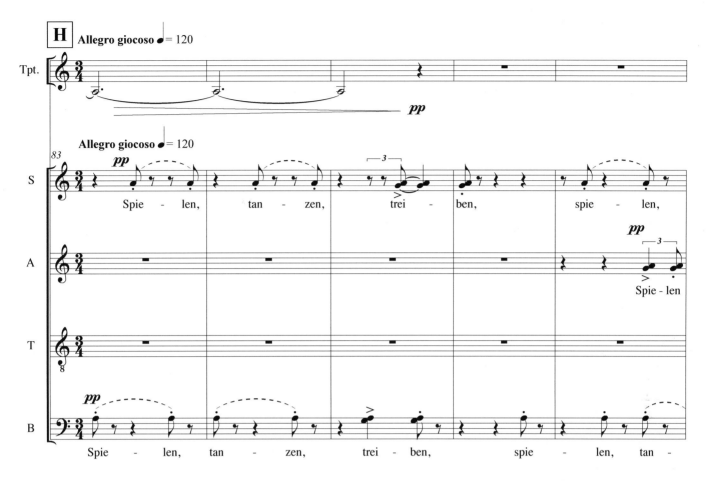

34841

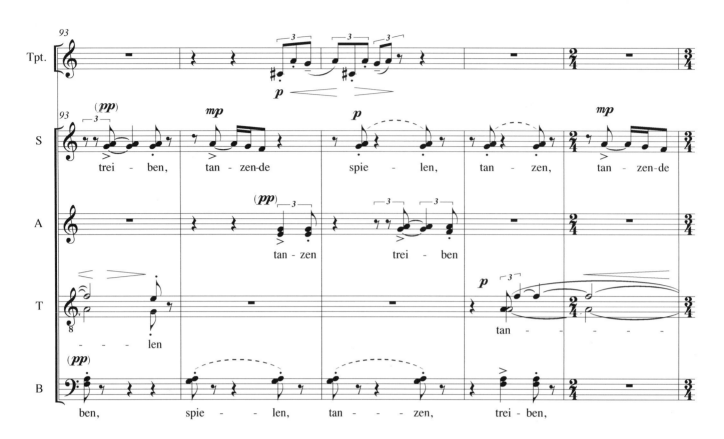

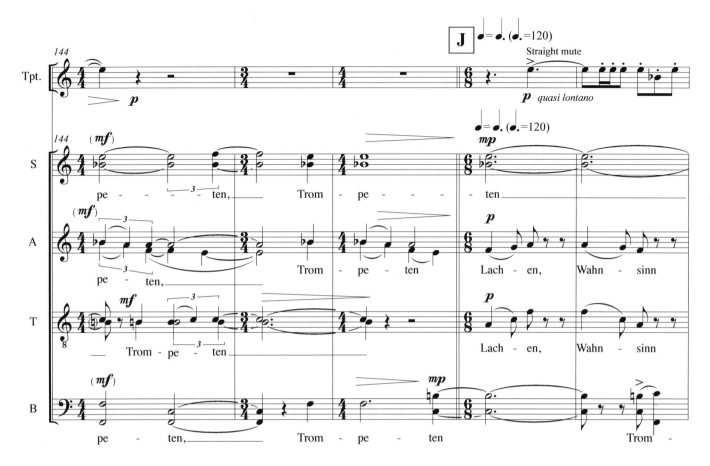

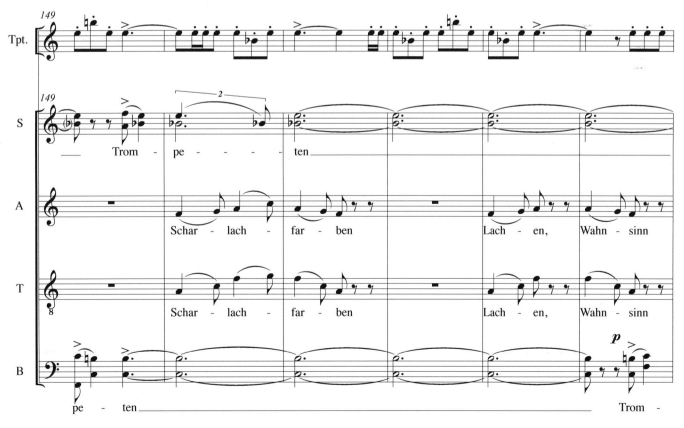

K

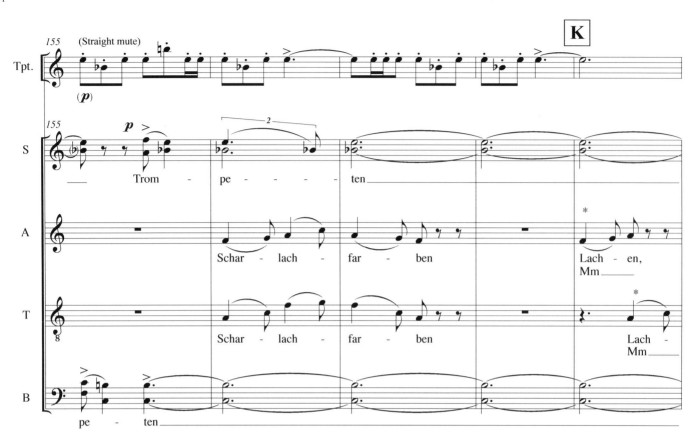

* From K towards the end, more and more altos and tenors should stop singing text and rather sing Mm as indicated. In bar 178-179, only one alto and one tenor should still be singing the text.

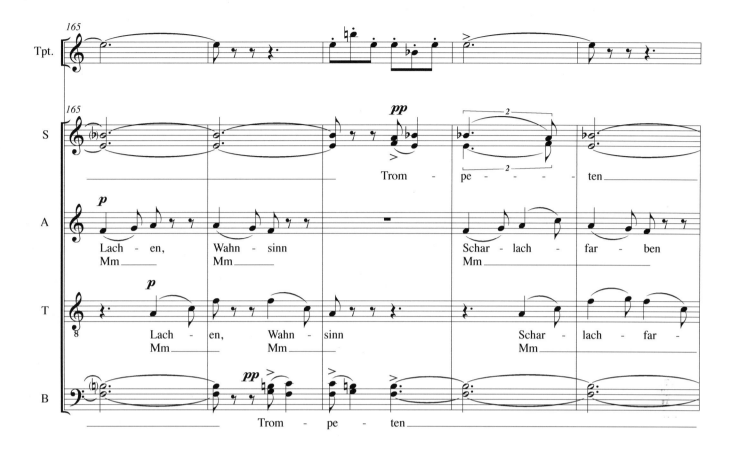

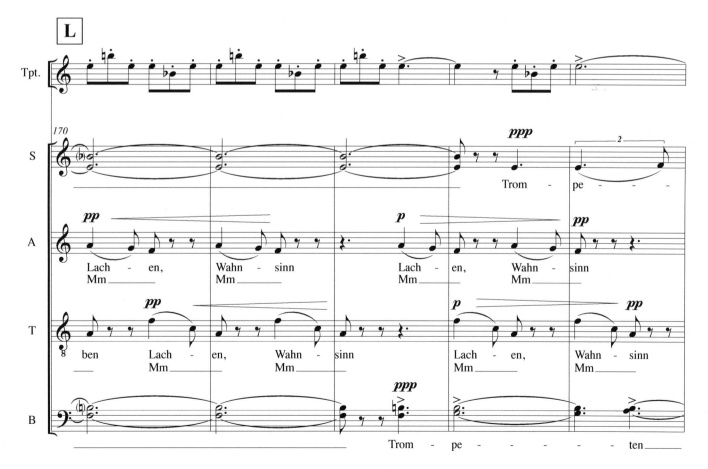

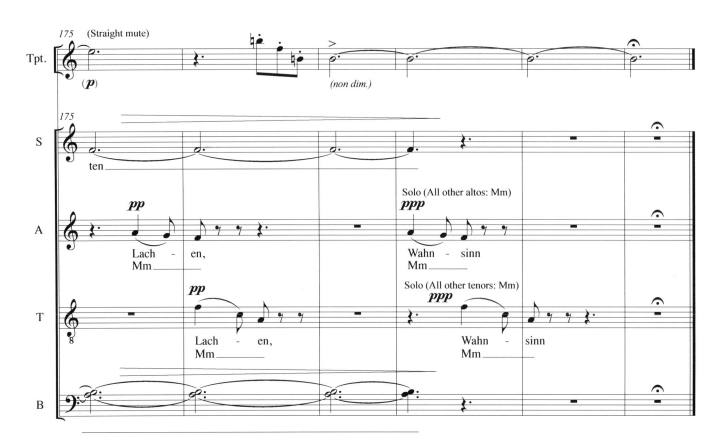

4. Interlude

* If sopranos and altos find the whistling notes in bar 13-18 too deep, they can be performed one octave up.

5. Nachts

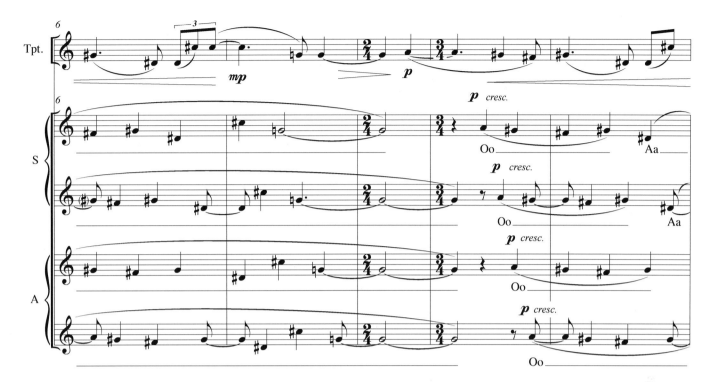

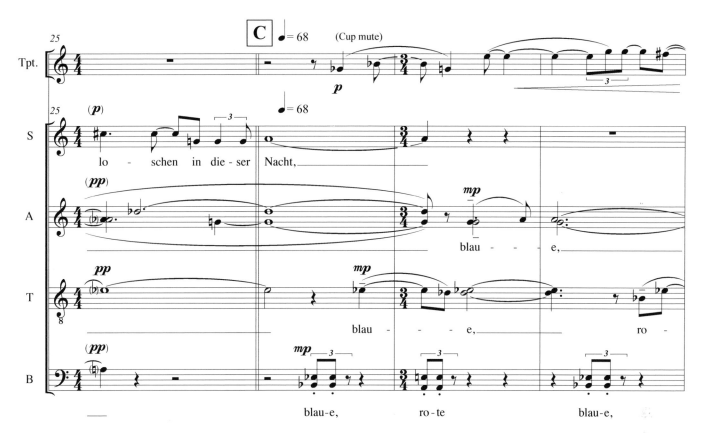

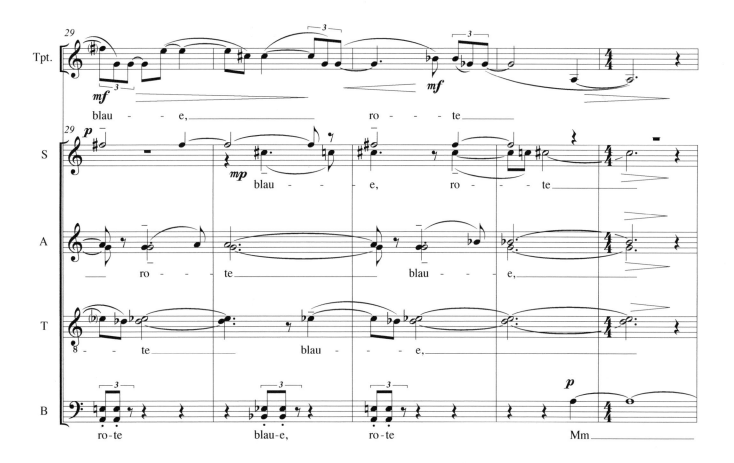

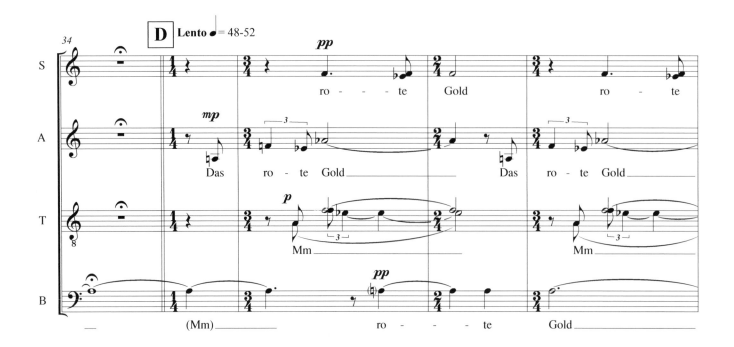

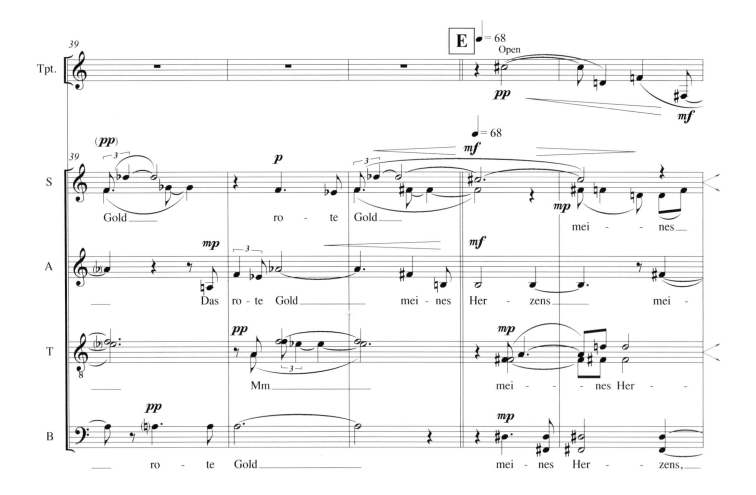

6. Untergang

* Sustained notes: sustain the *m* in im<u>m</u>er, *ng* or *n* in kli<u>ng</u>en.

* One singer (S, A, T or B) imitates a ticking clock by clicking his/her tongue. If only eight singers, the "Clock" part can be omitted.

34841

66

34841

68

* Sing sustainded r-sound (r in Gräber) to mimic the flutter tongue in the solo trumpet part.

** Repeat text as fast as possible (sempre p).

* Sing sustainded r-sound (*r* in Gräber) to mimic the flutter tongue in the solo trumpet part.

** Repeat text as fast as possible (sempre p)

75

34841

84

34841